**pa·tri·ot·ism** *noun, Br...*
devotion...

pa·tri·ot·isms

365 Heart-Warming Definitions to
Keep America's Renewed Sense of
National Pride and Patriotism Alive!

By Carole Marsh

Published by Gallopade International/Carole Marsh Books.
Printed in the United States of America!

Graphic Design and Editorial Assistant: Steven St. Laurent
Editorial Assistant: Rachel Moss

This book is typeset in Caslon Antique.
The first press-printing of the Declaration of Independence
was typeset—at Bejamin Franklin's request—in Caslon.

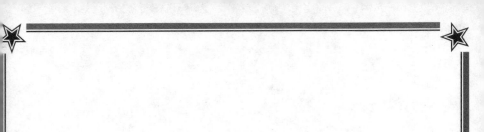

for Boom Pa,
with love

More Patriotic Titles by Carole Marsh:

- *Pa • tri • ot • isms* (companion to *The Daily Patriot*)

- Patriotic Favorites Coloring and Activity Book
- Young Patriot's Book of Puzzles, Games, Riddles, Stories, Poems, and Activities

- My American Flag to Color and Display! Activity Pack
- The Pledge of Allegiance Activity Pack
- America the Beautiful Activity
- The Star Spangled Banner Activity Pack

- The White House Christmas Mystery

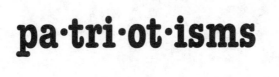

pa·tri·ot·isms

Patriotism is an attitude.
Get yours red, white, and blue.

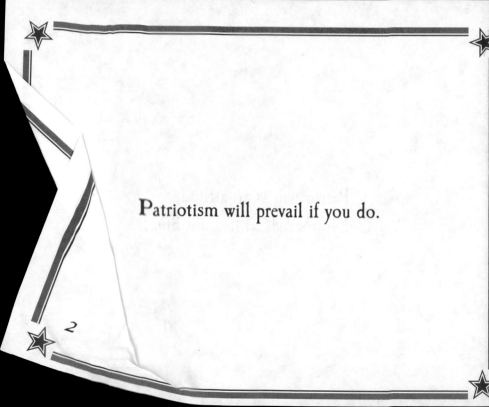

Patriotism will prevail if you do.

2

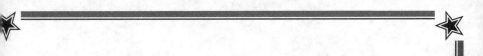

Patriotism is a reason, not a season.

Patriotism is love for one's country
in full bloom.

Patriotism is a poppy on a lapel,
and knowing why you wear it.

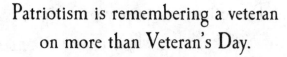

Patriotism is remembering a veteran
on more than Veteran's Day.

Patriotism is living for one's country, as well as dying for it, or being willing to do so.

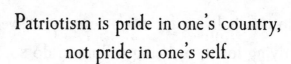

Patriotism is pride in one's country,
not pride in one's self.

Patriotism is a call to action.

Patriotism is truth-in-living.

Patriotism is remembering the past,
respecting the present,
and preparing for the future.

Patriotism is respect for all people.

Patriotism is having the ideal ideals.

13

Patriotism is service to one's nation.

Patriotism is defined by the people,
not the press.

Patriotism is not what you say,
it's what you do.

Patriotism and volunteerism are synonymous.

17

Patriotism is a true emotion;
it cannot be artificially summoned.

Patriotism is positive and optimistic.

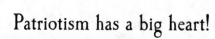

Patriotism has a big heart!

Patriotism is a promise to do better.

21

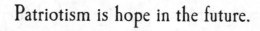

Patriotism is hope in the future.

Patriotism is belief in tomorrow.

Patriotism is a national treasure.

24

Patriotism is the heart of the people.

Patriotism is a tradition worth preserving.

Patriotism is awe and wonder at what is—
and what can be.

27

Patriotism is positive thinking.

Patriotism is a "can do" attitude.

Patriotism is taking part,
not copping out.

Patriotism is the reason
for the Fourth of July season!

31

Patriotism is faith in the future.

Patriotism is respect and remembrance.

33

Patriotism is duty and diligence.

Patriotism is as simple as picking up
litter that you didn't drop.

Patriotism is a worthwhile pursuit.

Patriotism is everyday citizenship.

Patriotism is belief in the best.

Patriotism is for and from the people.

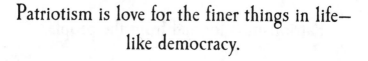

Patriotism is love for the finer things in life—
like democracy.

40

Patriotism is getting up instead of staying down.

41

Patriotism is comprehension of the value of a special way of life.

Patriotism is not self-righteousness . . .
. . . it is self-righting.

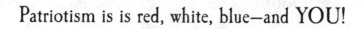

Patriotism is is red, white, blue—and YOU!

Patriotism is fireworks in the heart.

Patriotism is the soul of democracy.

Patriotism is an appreciation of peace,
and a willingness to defend it.

Patriotism is lending a hand . . . and a heart.

Patriotism is a red poppy on a blue lapel.

Patriotism is going to the National D-Day
Museum . . . and reading every display.

Patriotism is a color guard standing tall.

51

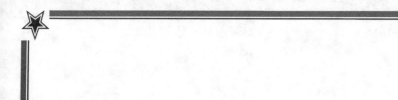

Patriotism is a veteran's smile.

Patriotism is a red, white, and blue cake . . .
. . . headed for a nursing home.

53

Patriotism is not pie in the sky,
it's the meat of the heart.

Patriotism is the freedom to start any business
you choose . . . and doing so.

55

Patriotism is an ongoing re-enactment
of the birth of the American soul.

Patriotism is the tears that always come
when you spy those endless rows
of little white crosses.

57

Patriotism is wanting to share democracy
with those deprived of it.

Patriotism is pleasure in small things . . .
. . . like a small child with his hand over his
heart saying the Pledge of Allegiance all wrong!

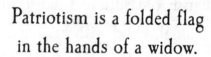

Patriotism is a folded flag
in the hands of a widow.

Patriotism is a baby decked out in
red, white, and blue bunting!

Patriotism is a six-year-old Uncle Sam
with long, blond, curly hair!

Patriotism is saying the Pledge of Allegiance . . .
. . . and meaning it Big Time!

Patriotism is not just talking the talk of
freedom, but walking the walk of freedom.

Patriotism is a contact sport:
Hug a veteran today!

Patriotism is a war hero who won a Purple Heart letting his grandkids call him Boom Pa.

Patriotism is a cherry pie . . . on its way to a veteran's home.

Patriotism is not cornball, it's "Play Ball!"

Patriotism is a yellow ribbon 'round a tree.

Patriotism is the American flag—
folded, furled, or flying high!

70

Patriotism is 50 stars that are best friends.

Patriotism is looking at, loving,
and sometimes laughing at those old
sepia-toned photographs of patriots of the past.
(You know: grandma, grandpa, etc.)

Patriotism is going to work
and not complaining about it.

73

Patriotism is red and white stripes
as bright as candy!

Patriotism is a whole pile of people
standing in a field on a hot summer's day
using their bodies to spell out FREEDOM.

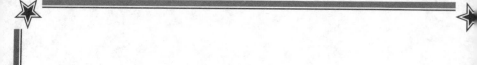

Patriotism is someone saying
"Iwo Jima" . . . and you knowing
that's not a make of automobile.

Patriotism is charitable.

Patriotism is generous.

Patriotism is joyful.

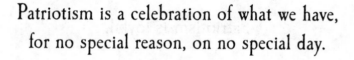

Patriotism is a celebration of what we have,
for no special reason, on no special day.

Patriotism is little hands holding little flags.

Patriotism is a parade of tissue-paper
floats with homemade signs.

Patriotism is any band playing patriotic music.
Out of key? Who cares?!

Patriotism is a pat on the back.

Patriotism is a red, white, and blue
quilt . . . covering a sleeping vet.

Patriotism is keeping the peace
while others are off fighting for it.

Patriotism is the freedom to live
anywhere you choose . . . and living there.

Patriotism is a farmer planting corn, growing corn, harvesting corn, selling corn . . . and donating corn to the hungry.

Patriotism is any ladle in any pot
dished out for a hungry soldier.

89

Patriotism is a Victory Garden in full bloom!

Patriotism is living in the land of the free
and the home of the brave—
and not taking it for granted.

Patriotism is reading a book
about America's history,
then sharing the story with a young person.

Patriotism is the lifeblood of the citizen.

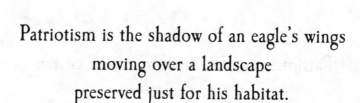

Patriotism is the shadow of an eagle's wings
moving over a landscape
preserved just for his habitat.

Patriotism is writing 100 times on the chalkboard: I LOVE MY COUNTRY! . . . because you want to.

Patriotism is a red, white, and blue teddy bear tucked into the arms of a sick child who won't live to serve her country.

Patriotism is the family of free men.

Patriotism is the dawn's early light . . .
shining over your home.

Patriotism is free speech; say something worthy!

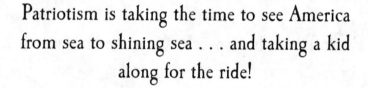

Patriotism is taking the time to see America from sea to shining sea . . . and taking a kid along for the ride!

Patriotism is a hard hat headed to work in
harm's way.

101

Patriotism is being the one left behind . . .
and not whining about it.

Patriotism is no trivial pursuit of happiness.

Patriotism is a wedding where the entire wedding party—even the bride—sport tiny flag pins on their finest bib and tucker duds!

Patriotism is a newborn baby named Freedom
or July or Dolley (as in Madison) . . . and her
growing up and loving it!

105

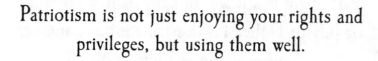

Patriotism is not just enjoying your rights and privileges, but using them well.

Patriotism is justice for all . . . starting with you.

107

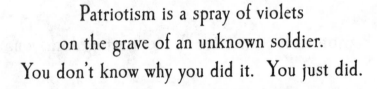

Patriotism is a spray of violets
on the grave of an unknown soldier.
You don't know why you did it. You just did.

Patriotism is the fifth of the four freedoms.

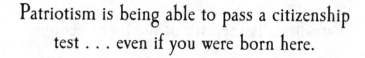

Patriotism is being able to pass a citizenship test . . . even if you were born here.

Patriotism is not just being American,
but acting like one.

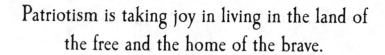

Patriotism is taking joy in living in the land of the free and the home of the brave.

Patriotism is doing your duty.
Maybe that's going off to war.
Maybe that's buying Girl Scout cookies.

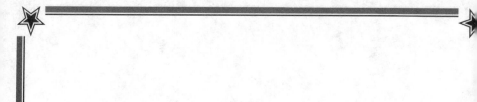

Patriotism is paying your taxes. (Really!)

Patriotism is your promise to preserve
democracy and freedom for the next generation.

115

Patriotism is a sticky note reminder to contribute to a good cause . . . and not throwing the sticky in the trash.

Patriotism is the opposite of a skull and crossbones, a swastika, a bad word— or anything close to these.

Patriotism is taking time to be thankful.

Patriotism is dropping bills, not coins, into the collection pot—wherever it may be.

119

Patriotism is taking a kid to a military
re-enactment . . . and explaining
what happened and why.

Patriotism is calling your Mom for no reason.
(Hey, these are my definitions.
If you don't like em, make up your own!)

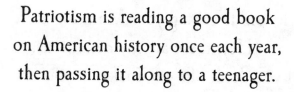

Patriotism is reading a good book
on American history once each year,
then passing it along to a teenager.

Patriotism is giving a helping hand,
or a handout—hey, whatever's called for.

123

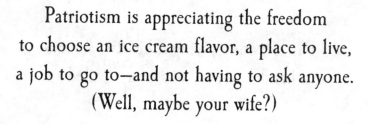

Patriotism is appreciating the freedom
to choose an ice cream flavor, a place to live,
a job to go to—and not having to ask anyone.
(Well, maybe your wife?)

Patriotism is knowing all the words
(in the right order, of course)
to the *Star-Spangled Banner*.

125

Patriotism is being in the parade,
or cheering on the parade: Take your choice!

Patriotism is not forgetting the soldiers
in your prayers . . . even after
the war is long over.

127

Patriotism is writing a Letter to the Editor,
then tearing it up if it's not positive.

Patriotism is not long-windedness,
it's long faithfulness.

129

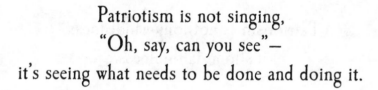

Patriotism is not singing,
"Oh, say, can you see"—
it's seeing what needs to be done and doing it.

130

Patriotism has nothing to do with politics.
Thank goodness!

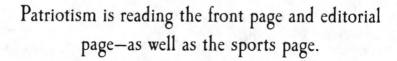

Patriotism is reading the front page and editorial page—as well as the sports page.

Patriotism is a light:
A candle's light at a vigil.
A flashlight at a Boy Scout all-nighter.
A lighthouse beacon steering a sailor safely
home from the sea.
It doesn't matter what the light is, or where.
It just matters that you keep it lit.

133

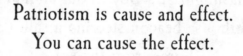

Patriotism is cause and effect.
You can cause the effect.

Patriotism is knowing at least a few of the names of those tiny islands in the Pacific. Americans died there for your freedom.

135

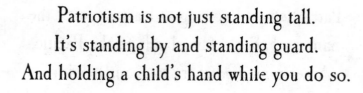

Patriotism is not just standing tall.
It's standing by and standing guard.
And holding a child's hand while you do so.

Patriotism is a bike-a-thon, a can-a-thon,
a tele-thon . . . whatever it takes
to get the job done.

137

Patriotism is a 5K, a 10K, a 401K—
whatever it takes. Freedom ain't free!

Patriotism is not thinking that social security
is sitting down to drink a beer.

139

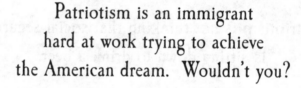

Patriotism is an immigrant
hard at work trying to achieve
the American dream. Wouldn't you?

Patriotism is being nice to a taxi driver.

141

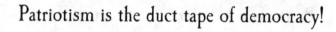

Patriotism is the duct tape of democracy!

Patriotism is a red, white, and blue yo-yo
that sings *Yankee Doodle Dandy*!

143

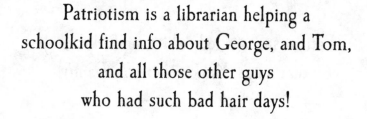

Patriotism is a librarian helping a
schoolkid find info about George, and Tom,
and all those other guys
who had such bad hair days!

Patriotism is keeping a stack of greeting cards
to send to those who have no one
to receive one from but you.

145

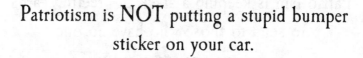

Patriotism is NOT putting a stupid bumper sticker on your car.

146

Patriotism is reading a book
to a kindergarten class—even if you're
six feet tall, male, a CEO, or famous.

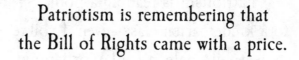

Patriotism is remembering that
the Bill of Rights came with a price.

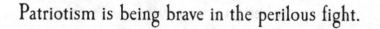

Patriotism is being brave in the perilous fight.

149

Patriotism is never forgetting Pearl Harbor,
September 11th, or any of those other
"days that were different."

Patriotism is sharing a banner crop, a banner year, or a banner life with those less fortunate.

Patriotism is decorating on Decoration Day.
(If you don't know when that is, look it up!)

Patriotism is a picnic.
(It's ok for patriotism to be a simple pleasure!)

Patriotism is a sack of groceries
headed for the homeless food pantry
instead of your kitchen.

Patriotism is knowing flag etiquette,
using it, and educating others.

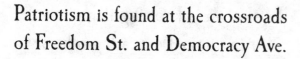

Patriotism is found at the crossroads
of Freedom St. and Democracy Ave.

Patriotism is taking your hat off
for the national anthem,
putting your hand over your heart,
singing out loud . . . and not wearing
a tank top to the ball game.

157

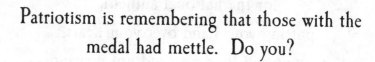

Patriotism is remembering that those with the
medal had mettle. Do you?

Patriotism is helping make sure that the bad history doesn't repeat itself.

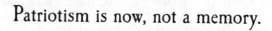

Patriotism is now, not a memory.

Patriotism is God blessing America
and you passing the blessing along.

161

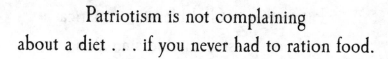

Patriotism is not complaining
about a diet . . . if you never had to ration food.

Patriotism is respect for the military instead of
Monday-morning quarterbacking them.

163

Patriotism is making sure
that you don't glorify war to young people.

Patriotism is not being a redneck,
unless you're someone who happens to work
in the hot sun all day long everyday.

165

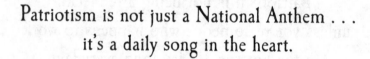

Patriotism is not just a National Anthem . . .
it's a daily song in the heart.

Patriotism is not a souvenir;
it's a saving grace.

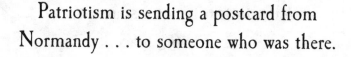

Patriotism is sending a postcard from
Normandy . . . to someone who was there.

Patriotism is being absolutely WOWED!
that 50 states get along so well for so long,
when some countries can't be good neighbors
for five minutes.

Patriotism is knowing that when you put your head on your pillow you know that you are sleeping in the best place on earth.

Patriotism is razzle-dazzle, razzmatazz,
and really hard work.

Patriotism is voting.
They're synonyms.
Get it?
Do it!

Patriotism is glory in the little things of freedom—like waking up free each day. (This one's for Chuck: "Do it again!")

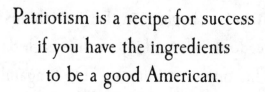

Patriotism is a recipe for success
if you have the ingredients
to be a good American.

Patriotism is a home run for freedom!

Patriotism is baking an Americake.
I don't know what that is,
but I'm certain it's delicious!

Patriotism is not just passing the hat . . .
it's putting something in it.

Patriotism is strawberries, blueberries,
and whipped cream hand-stacked into a
red, white, and blue arrangement
by a six-year-old. Trust me on this!

Patriotism is appreciating the Melting Pot.

179

Patriotism comes in all sizes, flavors, and ages.
We're not a one-nation-fits-all.
That's why we have new laws all the time.

Patriotism is not the majority, or the minority, or the majority minority. It's just us.

Patriotism is a hand-sewn flag
and a gentle kiss
on the needle-punctured fingers
that made it.

Patriotism is three cheers
for the red, white, and blue!
(A patriot is not shy!)

Patriotism is taking the time to share a box of mementos, and memories, with a vet.

Patriotism is getting a well-worn red
Jell-O star from a child . . . and eating it
with a smile on your face.

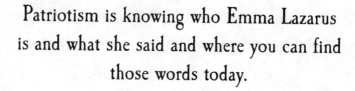

Patriotism is knowing who Emma Lazarus is and what she said and where you can find those words today.

Patriotism is a clean T-shirt that says something
about America that you wouldn't mind your
grandma reading.

187

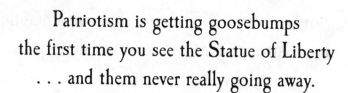

Patriotism is getting goosebumps
the first time you see the Statue of Liberty
. . . and them never really going away.

Patriotism is fresh Black-eyed Susans
on a sick veteran's nightstand.

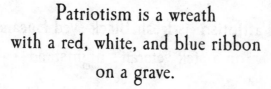

Patriotism is a wreath
with a red, white, and blue ribbon
on a grave.

190

Patriotism is deserving your democracy.

191

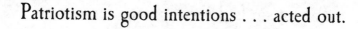

Patriotism is good intentions . . . acted out.

Patriotism is exercising your freedom
. . . more than at the gym.

Patriotism is the smell of barbecue ribs
grilling in *your* backyard!

Patriotism is being a good neighbor—
at home, and around the world.

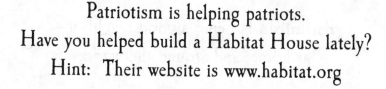

Patriotism is helping patriots.
Have you helped build a Habitat House lately?
Hint: Their website is www.habitat.org

Patriotism is popcorn, peanuts,
and Cracker Jack—best eaten with a veteran.
(P.S.: You don't have to go to the ballpark.)

Patriotism is taking a kid to the new National
Museum of Patriotism when it opens in 2004.
You'll enjoy it yourself!

Patriotism isn't a game;
it's a gameplan.

Patriotism is knowing the name of the President,
Vice President, Secretary of State,
Secretary of Defense, etc.—
no matter which party they belong to.

Patriotism is not drinking and driving
on the fourth . . . so everyone can be around
for the fifth, and the sixth, and . . .

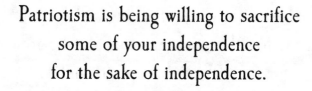

Patriotism is being willing to sacrifice
some of your independence
for the sake of independence.

Patriotism is not relegating veterans
to the antique roadshow!

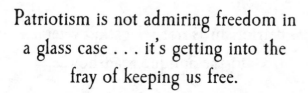

Patriotism is not admiring freedom in
a glass case . . . it's getting into the
fray of keeping us free.

Patriotism is a salute to all those who made—
and make—freedom possible.

Patriotism is not a fad; it's timeless.

Patriotism is as ageless as the past,
as contemporary as the present,
and as priceless as the future.

207

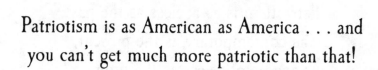

Patriotism is as American as America . . . and you can't get much more patriotic than that!

Patriotism isn't crucial, but it's useful.
Can you really imagine American life without it?

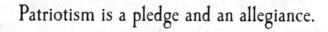

Patriotism is a pledge and an allegiance.

Patriotism is a many-splendored thing
and a many-layered emotion.

Patriotism is not a daydream;
it's the dream of a day when all people are free.

Patriotism is the garnish of democracy.

213

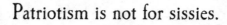

Patriotism is not for sissies.

Patriotism is not about a uniform,
it's about a form of unity.

Patriotism is hearing a call and heeding it.

Patriotism is not like Hollywood.
It isn't just glitter; it's gumption.

Patriotism in its purest form is a joy to observe.

Patriotism *is* the principle of the thing.

Patriotism is not greed, it's a creed.

Patriotism is the ideal emotion
for the ocean of ideals it tries to honor.

221

Patriotism is old-fashioned, newfangled,
and never goes out of style!

Patriotism is a choice.
Choose to feel great about your great nation!

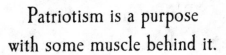

Patriotism is a purpose
with some muscle behind it.

Patriotism is character, or a character,
or part of the content of one's character.
Whichever, it's a character trait worth having.

225

Patriotism is not about *where* you are born,
it's about what you *do* where you're born.

Patriotism is ingenuity and integrity
in citizenship.

Patriotism is best expressed
with joy and dignity.
Jumping up and down is ok, too.

Patriotism is the handkerchief
he took to war saved intact
for the great, great, great grandchild,
and beyond.

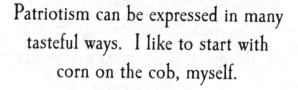

Patriotism can be expressed in many
tasteful ways. I like to start with
corn on the cob, myself.

230

Patriotism was born in the U.S.A.

231

Patriotism is not about lollygagging,
it's about loyalty.

Patriotism is creative;
even a great country can
always use some tweaking.

233

Patriotism is a gourmet batter of the following ingredients: one part love, one part loyalty, one part going, one part coming, and one part staying. Spice with enthusiasm and effort. Spread around joyfully. Bake in the warm sun until a flag stuck in the center holds firm. Serve early and often to all. Sometimes full of calories. Almost always cholesterol-heart-stopping wonderful!

Patriotism is as American as apple pie.
Or blueberry or blackberry.
Buttermilk. Rhubarb.
Chess. Sweet potato.
Banana cream.
Peach.
Etc. Etc. Etc.

235

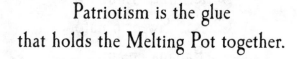

Patriotism is the glue
that holds the Melting Pot together.

Patriotism is a lotta little girls with a lotta red, white, and blue beads making a lotta beaded bracelets for a lotta good causes . . . and having a whole lotta fun doing it!

237

Patriotism can move your heart, move your hands, and move your mind, all for the best.

Patriotism is a way to share the spirit!

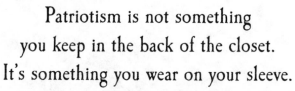

Patriotism is not something
you keep in the back of the closet.
It's something you wear on your sleeve.
It might say:
US Army . . .
EMS . . .
NYPD or FDNY . . .
Red Cross . . .

Patriotism is accessory after the fact of
freedom—everyone wants to be found guilty!

Patriotism is brave, not faint-hearted.

Patriotism is full of differences and diversity,
just like America.

243

Patriotism is Americans looking in the mirror
and liking what they see.

Patriotism is a symbol
that something's going right.

245

Patriotism is a parachute—
open against a blue sky, or closed forever,
having served its patriotic purpose.

Patriotism is a passion
for one's beloved homeland.

Patriotism does not put the country before the people. It can't. The people are the country.

Patriotism is not very patriotic
if it's not sacrificial.

249

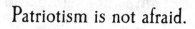

Patriotism is not afraid.

Patriotism is holding hands
with democracy and freedom.

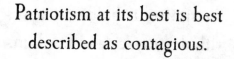

Patriotism at its best is best
described as contagious.

Patriotism is an embroidery,
with each of us serving as a stitch.

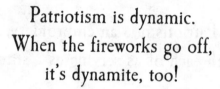

Patriotism is dynamic.
When the fireworks go off,
it's dynamite, too!

254

Patriotism is persnickety.
It wants the country to be just right.

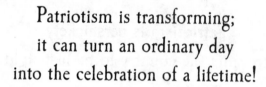

Patriotism is transforming;
it can turn an ordinary day
into the celebration of a lifetime!

Patriotism is being glad that a missing soldier
you'd never heard of is no longer missing.

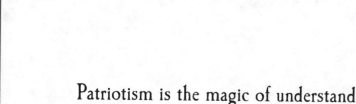

Patriotism is the magic of understanding
that it took a lot of blood, sweat, and tears
to create America . . . and having that make
you smile with pride.

Patriotism is victory in expressing
your love for your country.

Patriotism is respectful and respectable.
It does not gloat.
It does not embarrass.
It's something you would invite home
to meet your mother.

Patriotism is a vintage emotion—
and every year is a good vintage.

261

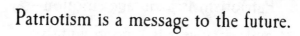

Patriotism is a message to the future.

Patriotism is enterprising—
it thinks of ways to do, not to undo.

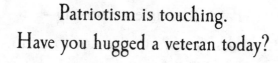

Patriotism is touching.
Have you hugged a veteran today?

Patriotism is a pattern.
If you follow it, you build
a habit of good citizenship.

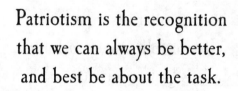

Patriotism is the recognition
that we can always be better,
and best be about the task.

Patriotism is a personal visit to every era of American history—and you never have to leave your seat in front of the U.S. Marine Band!

Patriotism is participation.
You don't have to "Join Up" to join up.

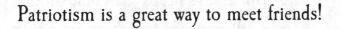

Patriotism is a great way to meet friends!

269

Patriotism always keeps marching along
over hill and dale and dusty trail.

Patriotism is cleaning out the porta-potty
at the Fourth of July celebration.
Thank you, whoever you are!

Patriotism is a slam dunk
through the hoop of freedom!

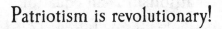

Patriotism is revolutionary!

273

Patriotism is an equation
that adds up to July 4, 1776!

Patriotism is eating homemade peach ice cream
out of a red bowl with a blue spoon.

275

Patriotism is the perfect gift.
Give it to your country today.

Patriotism is not about rednecks,
whitewash, or blueblood.
At its best, it comes in no color at all.

277

Patriotism is like jellybeans in a jar.
You can count the many ways you can be
patriotic, but still find at least one other reason
later beneath a sofa cushion.

Patriotism is a lifetime rally around the flag!

Patriotism separates the men from the boys.
Real men do love, cherish, and honor
their country.

Patriotism is the grand finale
to any celebration!

Patriotism is waving your flag,
tooting your horn, and getting your butt out
there to help do whatever needs doing.

Patriotism is a gigantic red watermelon
that never runs out—
no matter how large the crowd!

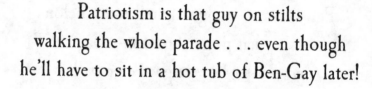

Patriotism is that guy on stilts
walking the whole parade . . . even though
he'll have to sit in a hot tub of Ben-Gay later!

Patriotism is never spoiled by
rain, sleet, snow, or no-shows!

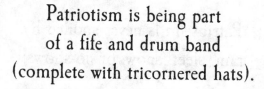

Patriotism is being part
of a fife and drum band
(complete with tricornered hats).

Patriotism is a basic food group.
We eat it up and come back for more!

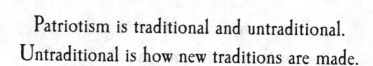

Patriotism is traditional and untraditional.
Untraditional is how new traditions are made.

288

Patriotism is always surprising—like America!

Patriotism is freedom of choice.
I think I'll have seconds, please.

Patriotism is not worrying how you say or spell
"Hurrah!" or "Hooray!"
It's just hurrahing and hooraying.

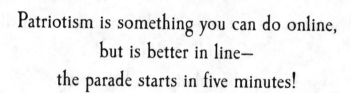

Patriotism is something you can do online,
but is better in line—
the parade starts in five minutes!

Patriotism is a bouquet of flowers—each
expressing the flowering of their patriotism in
their own way.

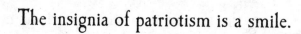

The insignia of patriotism is a smile.

Patriotism is an all-out campaign
against being a boring and apathetic citizen.

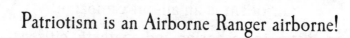

Patriotism is an Airborne Ranger airborne!

Patriotism is like a peanut butter and jelly
sandwich spread from the mountains
to the prairies to the oceans white with
marshmallow foam.

297

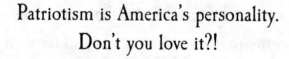

Patriotism is America's personality.
Don't you love it?!

Patriotism is Rosa Parks on a bus in Alabama.

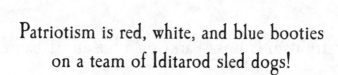

Patriotism is red, white, and blue booties
on a team of Iditarod sled dogs!

Patriotism is going to Arizona
to see the Grand Canyon!

Patriotism is playing a fiddle—
made in Arkansas, of course!

Patriotism is a non-stop flight—around the world—from and to Edwards Air Force Base, California.

303

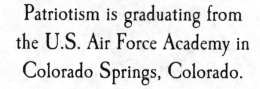

Patriotism is graduating from
the U.S. Air Force Academy in
Colorado Springs, Colorado.

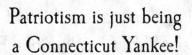

Patriotism is just being
a Connecticut Yankee!

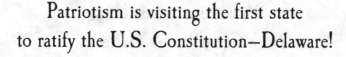

Patriotism is visiting the first state
to ratify the U.S. Constitution—Delaware!

Patriotism is Dolley Madison standing her
ground in the Disctrict of Columbia.

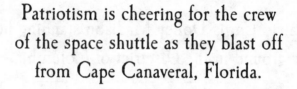

Patriotism is cheering for the crew
of the space shuttle as they blast off
from Cape Canaveral, Florida.

Patriotism is starting the long hike
up the Appalachian Trail from
Springer Mountain, Georgia.

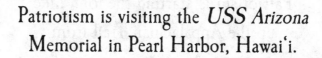

Patriotism is visiting the *USS Arizona* Memorial in Pearl Harbor, Hawai'i.

Patriotism is being proud
of our Idaho potatoes!

Patriotism is riding the Ferris wheel
at the Illinois State Fair.

Patriotism is a buggy ride
on the backroads of Indiana.

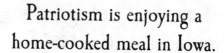

Patriotism is enjoying a
home-cooked meal in Iowa.

Patriotism is going to see the roses bloom in
Memorial Rose Garden, Riverside Park, Kansas.
They're there to honor those who
have died for our country!

315

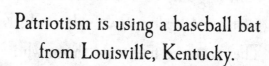

Patriotism is using a baseball bat
from Louisville, Kentucky.

Patriotism is negotiating the biggest land deal in history and doubling the size of the United States! (That was the Louisiana Purchase!)

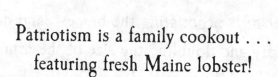

Patriotism is a family cookout . . .
featuring fresh Maine lobster!

Patriotism is the broad stripes and bright stars
of that star-spangled banner waving from the
ramparts of Fort McHenry, Maryland!

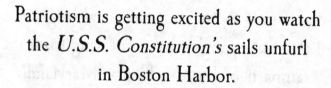

Patriotism is getting excited as you watch
the *U.S.S. Constitution's* sails unfurl
in Boston Harbor.

Patriotism is buying a car from
Detriot, Michigan.

Patriotism is believing in Paul Bunyan
and Babe the Blue Ox (who made all
the lakes in Minnesota)!

Patriotism is a Mississippi Riverboat
decked out from smokestack to paddlewheel
in red, white, and blue bunting!

Patriotism is a trip to the top of
the Gateway Arch in St. Louis, Missouri.

Patriotism is understanding why Montana
is called "Big Sky Country"!

Patriotism is a helpful 911 dispatcher
in Lincoln, Nebraska.

Patriotism is visiting Nevada . . . just for
the incredible scenery!

Patriotism is going to New Hampshire and earning a "This Car Climbed Mt. Washington!" bumper sticker for your car!

Patriotism is a troop of Boy Scouts
from New Jersey.

Patriotism is adding red chile peppers
from New Mexico to your chili!

Patriotism is standing tall and proud
on Liberty Island in New York Harbor!

331

Patriotism is Orville Wright
making a 12-second flight across the sand
at Kill Devil Hills, North Carolina.

Patriotism is visiting the International Peace
Garden near Dunseith, North Dakota.

333

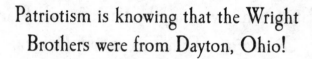

Patriotism is knowing that the Wright
Brothers were from Dayton, Ohio!

Patriotism is an American flag
flying at the front door of a real
Native American's home in Oklahoma.

335

Patriotism is visting Fort Clatsop, Oregon,
and wanting to follow the trail that
Lewis & Clark blazed!

Patriotism is seeing the Liberty Bell in
Philadelphia, Pennsylvania—
and understanding its significance.

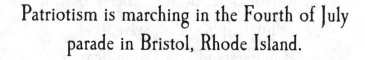

Patriotism is marching in the Fourth of July
parade in Bristol, Rhode Island.

Patriotism is the flag of the **United** States
flying over Fort Sumter, South Carolina.

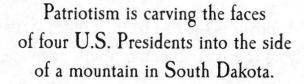

Patriotism is carving the faces
of four U.S. Presidents into the side
of a mountain in South Dakota.

Patriotism sings in Nashville, Tennessee!

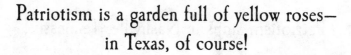

Patriotism is a garden full of yellow roses—
in Texas, of course!

Patriotism is carrying a torn and tattered
American flag at the Winter Olympics'
Opening Ceremonies in Salt Lake City, Utah.

343

Patriotism is tasting a fresh batch of
maple syrup in Vermont.

Patriotism is everywhere in Virginia:
Jamestown, Williamsburg, Mount Vernon,
and—especially—Arlington!

Patriotism is a sailor taking the helm of a
Coast Guard Motor Lifeboat at Cape
Disappointment, Washington.

Patriotism is an American flag sticker
on a West Virginia coal miner's hardhat.

347

Patriotism is a proud Wisconsin cheesehead!

Patriotism is as Faithful as that Old geyser in
Yellowstone National Park, Wyoming.

Patriotism is 50 states stitched together
into an inseparable quilt.

Patriotism is getting along with your next-door neighbor—especially when it's a nation!

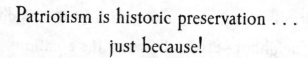

Patriotism is historic preservation . . .
just because!

Patriotism is keeping the lighthouse light lit.

Patriotism is keeping the home fires burning . . .
for as long as it takes.

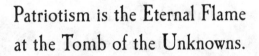

Patriotism is the Eternal Flame
at the Tomb of the Unknowns.

355

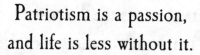

Patriotism is a passion,
and life is less without it.

Patriotism is a Care Package to a soldier.

Patriotism is addictive!

Patriotism is so . . . so . . . so patriotic!

Patriotism should never end.